The Heart of Boston Rap

5) When Ritchie announced that the next rap was called the *Heart of Boston Rap*, he raised Sarah's arm to show that she had written it.

____

____

5) Ritchie's final rap was about love.

____

____

6) When Ritchie said 'Go!', the others in the band didn't know what he meant.

____

____

7) The final song played by *Dire Straits Recovered* was *Sultans of Swing*.

____

____

CHAPTER 15

Working in groups of 11–12, prepare to perform the scenes in the chapter. Assign the roles and learn your lines. One member of the group should be the director.

CHAPTER 16

Read through the chapter carefully, then put your book aside and take a close look at the following sentences. Each of them contains one word that is not in the original text. Cross out the extra word. When finished, check your answers.

1) *Aware that they were staring at me, I searched for something – anything – to say.*
2) *I felt like a diver on a very high rock looking down at the dark water below.*
3) *Just then, two huge security men came over to us.*
4) *I know Mrs. Timmins and I know that she loves Mattapan just as much as Ritchie does, too.*
5) *Normally, all Ritchie has to do is snap his fingers and all the girls come running.*
6) *Scooter nodded slowly, his sharp eyes fixed on mine.*
7) *'Come on, Sarah, spit it out!'*

CHAPTER 17

In groups of six, assign roles and prepare and give a performance of the final scene.

Dwain Pickett

The Heart of Boston Rap

Ernst Klett Sprachen
Stuttgart

1. Auflage 1 11 10 9 8 7 | 2025 24 23 22 21

Internetadresse: www.klett-sprachen.de

Zeichnungen: Sven Palmowski, Barcelona
Redaktion: Paul Newcomb
Layoutkonzeption: Elmar Feuerbach
Gestaltung und Satz: Satzkasten, Stuttgart
Umschlaggestaltung: Elmar Feuerbach
Titelbild: Thinkstock (Hemera), München
Druck und Bindung: CEWE Stiftung & Co. KGaA, Germering

Printed in Germany

ISBN 978-3-12-542605-4

Contents

Abbreviations used in notes

abb	abbreviation
AE	American English
coll	colloquial
esp	especially
inf	informal
opp	opposite
sb	somebody
sth	something
sl	slang
vulg	vulgar

About This Book

This book is a work of fiction. The characters, incidents, and dialogs are products of my imagination. Any resemblance to actual events or persons, living or dead, is entirely unintentional.

I want to say a word about two of the raps that play an important role in the story.

First of all, it must be said that it is normal for raps to rap (criticize) things. The rap about Boston, The Heart of Boston Rap, and the rap called Mattapan are typically critical. The many negative things said about Boston do not, however, reflect my opinion. I love Boston. To my mind, Boston is a great place to visit (or to live in).

As far as the rap about the community of Mattapan is concerned, it is true that Mattapan has a bad reputation for violent crime. The reasons why Mattapan is so different from the rest of Boston are obvious: firstly, Mattapan is part of a city that is one of the ten safest in the U.S., in a state (Massachusetts) that is ranked among the safer states, and secondly, a few spectacular crimes in Mattapan have attracted nationwide attention. But Mattapan is not as bad as its image. In fact, lots of things are happening to improve the quality of life in Mattapan, including the building of the multi-million dollar Mattapan Branch Library.

Finally, in the Activities (chapters 4, 5, 10) you, the student, will have the opportunity of becoming a rapper in rap contests! If you prefer a less active role, you can be part of the jury.

Throughout the book, spelling and phonemic transcriptions are in standard American English.

Dwain Pickett

WHAT DO YOU DO WHEN YOUR BEST FRIEND IS MAKING A BAD MISTAKE?

1
Sleepwalker

What do you do when your best friend is making a bad mistake?

My best friend Alicia has got a new boyfriend, Ritchie Timmons. When she talks about him – and that's often, believe me – she gets this dreamy grin on her face. He's her first like serious boyfriend.

I don't like this. Alicia is a Senior at South Boston High, one of Boston's best high schools, headed for college. Ritchie is a school dropout, headed nowhere. She lives in a beautiful bungalow near ours in an upper middle-class neighborhood, he in a rundown apartment building in what the press calls the most dangerous district in the city.

Don't get me wrong. Ritchie is a good looking guy, tall and naturally well built – not in that bodybuilder way. With his bright smile and deep, warm voice he can also be very charming. I've got nothing against him personally. But you have to be realistic about things like this. There are too many differences between him and Alicia. She's heading for a broken heart.

Still, sometimes I think I should leave her alone and let her go her own way, whatever happens. After all, she has made it clear that she doesn't want me 'sticking my nose in her business', as she puts it. So why should I bother? It's a no-win situation for me.

But then I ask myself, what if I was Alicia? I'd probably say I want to be left alone, too. But deep down I'd hope that my friend would do what's best

7 **grin** a big, wide smile – 10 **to head for** to go towards – 27 **to stick your nose in sb's business** *inf* to try to know things about sb that they don't want you to know – 28 **to bother** to spend time or energy doing sth

for me. Alicia doesn't realize what's best for her. She's like a sleepwalker on top of a high building. What does a true friend do in a situation like that? Duh, sure, the true friend tries to stop her before she falls over the edge.

I'm walking a thin line. I've got to make her realize she's making a bad mistake, but I've got to be careful about how I do it. If I say too much, she'll get angry and cut me out. I have to try to keep our lines of communication open. It's the only way I can know what's going on and be able to help her.

Oh, I forgot to mention it – Ritchie's other name is Ritchie T. He's a rapper.

4 **duh** *inf, sl* of course, you idiot! – 9 **to cut sb out** *inf* to stop having anything to do with sb – 12 **to mention** to say (by chance)

2
Count me in!

Ritchie waited for Alicia almost every day after school. He was very cool about it, always busy with his cell phone, looking like the busiest guy in the world. To me, it was laughable, but Alicia didn't seem to notice that it was all a big act. She was too happy to see him to notice anything like that.

Today was different. Ritchie's cell phone was in his pocket. In fact, he was looking at Alicia and smiling all over his face when she appeared. As usual, he only had eyes for her. That was fine with me. In fact, I couldn't care less if he noticed me or not.

He took her in his arms and gave her a kiss. It was a quick kiss because he had something important to say and couldn't wait.

'You remember I told you about entering that contest? The one for rappers? Well, I won it!'

I knew immediately what he was talking about. It was the city of Boston's annual Calling all Rappers contest. It was open to everyone. A jury of famous rappers that included Termanology, Sev-One and Mr. Lif chose the best rap.

Alicia shook her head. 'You – you did?' She couldn't seem to believe what she was hearing.

'Yeah, is that so surprising?'

'No, no. Of course not. Hey, that's great!'

'Great? It's more than great! It's – it's fantastic! Did I tell you what the first prize is?'

'Er, no.'

'First prize is a professionally made video production!'

7 **act** a façade, not real – 13 **I couldn't care less** *inf* "I don't think that's important at all." – 18 **to enter** to put your name on the list for – 21 **annual** [ˈænjuəl] every year

Alicia nodded but it was obvious that she didn't know what he was talking about.

Ritchie laughed. 'A professional video-making team complete with cameraman, lighting person, storyboard artist and director are going to help me make a video with my prize-winning rap. In their studio – a whole day!'

Now Alicia understood. 'Oh, Ritchie!' She threw herself in his arms.

Ritchie held her a moment, then took a step back. There was a playful look on his face. 'Of course, I need people to help me. You know, to take part in the video. And the first person I thought of was you!' he said

Alicia's eyes grew wide. 'Me?' she said, 'In a rap video? But Ritchie, you know I can't rap.'

'You won't have to rap. I do the rapping. You just have to look hot like you always do.'

Alicia's face turned red and she began to laugh. She looked at me, then turned to Ritchie. 'What about Sarah? Can she be in it, too?'

'Sarah? Sure, Sarah can be in it, too.'

'Alicia?' I said.

'Yeah?'

'You forgot to ask Sarah if she wants to be in the video.'

Alicia looked a little confused. She looked me in the eye, trying to understand what I meant. Then she gave a little laugh. 'Of course. Sorry. Would you like to take part in Ritchie's video?'

I didn't answer at once. I waited a moment to make it look like it was a hard decision. Finally, I said, 'I'm not sure. I – '

5 **storyboard artist** sb who draws pictures showing the scenes in a planned video or film – 18 **hot** *inf* sexy – 32 **decision** to make a ~ is to choose what you could or should do

‘Oh, come on, Sarah. You’ll like it, I know you will,’ Ritchie cut in.

I hesitated again. At last, I nodded and said, ‘Okay, count me in.’

Alicia looked at me with shining eyes. ‘Thanks, Sarah. That means a lot to me,’ she said.

Suddenly, Ritchie took the two of us by the hand. ‘This’ll be fun, girls, and – who knows? – if it’s good and gets clicked on a million times in YouTube, it could be the beginning of something big!’

Alicia’s mouth was wide open. I looked at Ritchie and rolled my eyes.

2 **to cut in** to say sth when sb is talking – 3 **to hesitate** to be slow to speak because you are uncertain or nervous – 5 **to shine** to be bright – 12 **to roll your eyes** to move your eyes in order to show you don’t believe sb

3
Ritchie's love rap

Alicia and I were on our way home from school the next day, Alicia driving, me sitting beside her. We were waiting on a red light. She had just said how excited she was about being in Ritchie's video. She couldn't wait till Saturday, the big day. When I only nodded, she gave me a sharp questioning look. 'Aren't you excited about it, too?' she said.

'Very excited,' I said.

She gave me another questioning look. 'You don't sound like it.'

'My God, what do you want me to do – burst into song?'

'Come on, Sarah, I know what you think about Ritchie. I know you don't like me going with him. But I thought this might change things.'

'This?'

'Him winning the contest, getting the chance to make a video and asking us to be part of it. Doesn't it mean anything to you?'

I nodded my head quickly. 'Of course it does. I think it's wonderful that he won the contest, and really sweet that he asked us to be in his video. It's just that – the whole thing – the rapper scene – it's not my world. And I don't think it's yours, either.'

Alicia's eyes flashed. 'Damn it, Sarah! Haven't we talked about this before? Haven't I made my position clear? If you want to be my friend, you'll have to accept certain things. Otherwise, you – you can find yourself a new friend.' Alicia was squeezing

13 **to burst into** to start doing sth suddenly – 27 **to flash** to become very bright for a short time – 27 **damn** [dæm] a word people use to show that they are angry *(Verdammt!)* – 30 **otherwise** used to say what the result would be if sth did not happen or the situation were different *(sonst)*

the steering wheel so hard that her fingers were white.

Uh-oh, I'd done it again. I'd crossed that line. I put my hand lightly on Alicia's shoulder. 'I'm sorry. I didn't mean that. I was running off at the mouth again.'

Alicia gave me a little smile but didn't say anything.

Just then, the red light turned green and we crossed the intersection.

Alicia looked straight ahead. She seemed to be concentrating on her driving, but her silence was making me nervous.

I tried to think of something to say. Finally, I looked at her and smiled. 'Do you know what the rap is about?'

5 **to run off at the mouth** *inf* to talk too much – 10 **intersection** a place where two or more roads meet – 12 **silence** no sound

'You mean the one for the video?'

'Yep.'

'I presume it'll be the same one he won the contest with – yeah, he showed it to me.' Alicia thought for a moment, then said, 'It's about love.'

I felt my face grow warm. 'Wow! A romantic rap. I didn't know Ritchie was like that.'

Alicia shook her head and laughed. 'He's not. It's not so much romantic. It's more like – uh, philosophical.'

'Philosophical?'

'Yeah, it's more like in school. Logical, you know. But it's too deep for me.'

Yeah, yeah, that was the Ritchie I knew. Not just a good looker, but also a deep thinker. Always asking questions, looking for answers. Not unlike myself. I had to smile.

Alicia turned into our street and slowed down. When she stopped in front of my house, she turned to me and said, 'You haven't said a word for the last five minutes. That's not like you. Is it because I got mad at you?'

I shook my head. 'No, no. I was, uh, thinking about that Math test tomorrow. It's making me nervous.'

'You'll do alright. You always do,' Alicia said, laughing.

I got out and shut the car door. I waved to her, then began walking around to the side door of our house. I was still thinking about Ritchie and his rap – the one about love.

21 **to get mad at sb** *sl* to become angry with sb

4
Making the video

The rest of the week went by quickly. On Saturday, I got up early and went for a long run. After breakfast, I hurried up to my room and put on the costume I had bought for the rap. The next ten minutes I spent putting on makeup. Finished, I took one last look in the mirror and smiled to myself. After that, I put the costume in a bag, got dressed and went downstairs to wait for Alicia. A few minutes later, she drove into our driveway. I said goodbye to mom and rushed out of the house. Alicia greeted me, her eyes wide with excitement. I was excited, too, but tried not to show it.

Ritchie and his band were already at the studio when Alicia and I arrived. They were in a small room practicing and didn't notice us.

A tall, thin, gray-haired man came up to us and introduced himself as Jay Bagnell, the sound engineer. He led us to a room at the back, a kitchen, where the video production team was having coffee. There he introduced us to the team: Jerry Webb, the director, Sydney Thomson, the camera man, Maria Cortez, in charge of the lighting and Andy Chapman, the storyboard artist. They were a young team, friendly and full of fun. Alicia and I had both been nervous, but after talking with them a few minutes, we were laughing so much that we forgot about being nervous.

After that, Jay – he insisted we had to call him and the others by their first names – took us to the room where Ritchie and the others were practicing. Alicia

5 **costume** the clothes worn in a film, video, etc. – 12 **to greet** to say hello (to sb) – 22 **to introduce** to tell people who haven't met before what each others' names are – 30 **to insist** to say that it must be done *(bestehen)*

and I sat quietly and listened. I knew Ritchie was a talented rapper, but I was surprised at how good he sounded together with his band.

When they finished, Ritchie came over and took Alicia in his arms. Then, surprisingly, he took me in his arms, too. Smiling, he introduced us to his 'brothers', as he called them. Rico was the dark, broad-shouldered one, Jackson the tall, thin guy and Scooter the even taller redhead. They only nodded, but they were friendly nods. Normally, Rico was Ritchie's guitarist, Jackson his drummer and Scooter his keyboard player. But today the music had been pre-recorded, leaving the three of them free to take part in the performance.

Just then, Jay came in and said it was time to get ready. The video shoot would begin in fifteen minutes. He took Alicia and me to a small room where we could get ready.

When I had changed into my costume, I noticed that Alicia was staring at me.

'Are you going to wear *that?*' she said.

I looked at my costume. 'Is there something wrong with it?' I said.

She shook her head and gave me a strange little smile. 'No, no, I'm just a little surprised you would wear something like that. It's, uh, very sexy.'

'Well, he told us to wear something sexy, didn't he?'

Alicia nodded slowly. 'Yeah, I guess you're right, but – whatever – I'm sure he and the others will like it.'

At the start of the shoot, Jerry called us together. He was holding a copy of Ritchie's rap in his hand.

13 **pre-recorded** put onto a CD before, (*opp* of live) – 14 **to take part in sth** to do sth together with other people *(an etwas teilnehmen)* – 16 **shoot** a period of time when a video, film, etc. is made – 30 **whatever** *inf* used to say that anything is acceptable

He read out the title: 'Love is a Nine-Letter Word'. He smiled at Ritchie and said, 'I like the title and I love the lyrics. Now I'm going to ask you and the others to perform the rap from beginning to end. Please don't stop, even if you make a mistake. I want to see what kind of performance you have come up with. That will give me a better idea of what we can do with it.'

'Right,' Ritchie said, then turned to us. 'Are you guys ready?'

Ritchie had given Alicia and me each a copy of the choreography for the video, and we'd practiced our parts together, so we knew what we had to do. We got in position beside Ritchie and the others. A moment later, from behind a large window in another room, Jay gave the signal to start and the beat began. Jerry was sitting beside him with his eyes fixed on us as Ritchie went up to the microphone and began to rap.

Love your brothers,
love your brothers,
you hear it every day,
Before *I* say
love your brothers,
I wanna know what love is,
I *gotta* know what love is.
But the *word* love is in the way,
it's used too much,
all screwed up.
Gotta get below the word,
deep down,
where the meaning lies,
shining like gold.

6 **to come up with** to think up, to create – 29 **to be screwed up** *inf* to be ruined

It’s promotion, man, promotion,
forward motion,
lifting things to a higher level,
a sky-high level!
Three steps are necessary,
one, two, three,
see the good,
say yeah to it and
support it all you can.
See, say, support,
the three steps,
the choreography
of the dance called love.

Love is a nine-letter word,
P-R-O-M-O-T-I-O-N,
promotion,
forward Motion,
see, say, support,
see, say, support
see the good,
say yeah to it, and
support it all you can, man!

Put that way
it sounds so easy,
a piece of cake, you say,
we *all* wanna be promoters, you say,
but believe this:
love’s a thin, thin line,
non-love a super highway!
Putting down’s
easier than lifting up,

1 **promotion** when you try to do sth to make sth more popular or successful – 2 **forward** [ˈfɔːrwɚd] towards a place or position that is in front – 3 **to lift** to move to a higher position – 10 **support** [səˈpɔːrt] help – 23 **put** here: said – 25 **a piece of cake** *inf* very easy – 30 **to put sb down** to make sb look silly

tearing down's
easier than building up.
Unkind words, the kind that hurt,
that leave you bleeding in the dirt,
silence that speaks a thousand words,
compliments not given,
thanks unspoken,
saying no or nothing at all,
the many lanes of non-love's super highway!
The guys who criticize
say nothing's worth supporting,
sit back and laugh,
smart-asses,
faultfinders,
nitpickers,
and know-it-alls.

Love is a nine-letter word,
P-R-O-M-O-T-I-O-N,
promotion is
forward Motion is
see, say, support,
see, say, support,
see the good,
affirm the good, and
support it all you can, man!

'Great stuff, guys. I like it!' We looked around. Jerry was coming toward us, giving us the thumbs up sign, and smiling from ear to ear.

1 **to tear down** to criticize sharply – 4 **dirt** [dɜːrt] the ground – 9 **lane** a highway has several ~s, e.g. a slow ~ and a fast ~ – 11 **worth** when sth is ~ doing, it is important or good enough to try to do – 13 **smart-ass** *inf, sl* clever person – 14 **faultfinder** a person who likes to find mistakes – 15 **nitpicker** a person who concentrates on small and unimportant details – 24 **to affirm** to say strongly that sth is true – 27 **thumbs up** a sign used to show that sth is good

5
Celebrating the video

'When Jerry said 'great stuff!' I thought that was all there was to it,' Ritchie said, laughing.

'Me, too,' Alicia said. 'I thought all they'd have to do was film it and we'd be on our way.'

I nodded. 'I was thinking the same thing.'

The three of us, Ritchie, Alicia and I, were sitting in The Gourmet Pizza, one of Boston's best pizzerias, nipping at our drinks and waiting for our pizzas. It was Alicia's idea – to celebrate the completion of the video. She was sitting beside Ritchie, I was opposite them. As usual, the place was crowded.

'But when he said 'great!', that was just the beginning,' said Ritchie.

'Yep. The beginning of eight hours of hard work!' I said.

Alicia smiled at me. 'Hard, but fun,' she said.

'Definitely!' I nodded and smiled back.

Ritchie shook his head. 'Working with the production team wasn't like working at all. It was – like, it was fun. The way they treated us – so respectfully. Not like they were the professionals and we the amateurs.'

'Yeah, they treated us as equals. Not like some teachers do,' said Alicia.

'And we learned so much – it was like a crash course,' I said.

Ritchie laughed. 'There was so much to it! I never thought a rap video could be so complicated.'

10 **to nip at** *(inf)* to drink a little at a time – 19 **definitely** a way of saying strongly that sth is true – 22 **to treat** if you ~ sb well, you are good to them – 25 **equal** if you treat sb as your ~, you think of them as just as important as yourself

Just then, the moment came we'd all been waiting for: our pizzas were ready! The tall, blonde waitress looked at Alicia and said, 'The Four Cheese Pizza is for you?'

Alicia nodded, and the waitress placed the steaming plate in front of her.

Looking at me, she said, 'And you ordered the – ?'

'The Extreme Mushroom Pizza,' I said.

'Here you are!' she said with a big smile, putting the plate in front of me.

Then she moved up close to Ritchie with a playful look in her eye. 'And you ordered the Spicy Chicken Pesto. Are you having it for the first time?'

'Yeah. Why do you ask?'

'It's my favorite but I've got to warn you: it's really hot!'

Ritchie laughed. 'Hot hot or spicy hot?'

'All of our pizza is hot hot. Our Spicy Chicken Pesto is hot hot *and* spicy hot.'

'That,' Ritchie said slowly, 'is exactly why I ordered it.' Smiling, he winked at her and added, 'But thanks for the warning.'

'You're welcome, good looking!' she said, winking back at him and turning to go.

Very little was said for the next few minutes, the time it takes hungry teens to finish off a pizza. Ritchie was through first. Smiling happily, he leaned back and loosened his belt. 'Getting back to the video,' he said, 'it was amazing what they did with our concept.'

'With *your* concept, the best ideas were yours,' Alicia said to Ritchie.

'Great ideas,' I added.

6 **to steam** *dampfen* – 17 **spicy** ['spaɪsi] (of food) *scharf (gewürzt)* – 21 **to wink** to close then open one eye quickly, often as a signal – 28 **to loosen** ['luːsən] if sth fits too closely to your body, you can ~ it to feel more comfortable – 28 **belt** *Gürtel* – 29 **amazing** very surprising

'Whatever,' said Ritchie, 'but they made the most of them. The first part – about me looking up the meaning of the word love, they put in a library setting. That was good!'

'With me as a student sitting near you, trying to catch your eye – ' Alicia began.

'And me as the librarian,' I cut in.

'The sexy librarian,' Ritchie said quickly, 'with glasses on her nose.' Ritchie started laughing but stopped when he noticed the look on Alicia's face.

'And then all three of us miming the three steps of the dance called love,' I said.

'Yeah, that was great,' said Ritchie. 'And I liked the next part, too, the refrain. You know? Love is a nine-letter word.'

'With you as the teacher,' Alicia said, turning to Ritchie, 'standing at the board with a pointer in your hand, pointing at the nine letters, one by one.'

'I was the one with glasses in that scene,' Ritchie said, smiling at me.

Alicia snuggled up closer to Ritchie. 'And then came the scene I liked best: the part about non-love, the catwalk scene,' she said.

'It was my favorite, too,' I said.

'Oh, yeah, it was brilliant!' Ritchie laughed. 'The 'models' as the victims, walking down the catwalk, heads high at first, but then hanging when I as the audience gave them the thumbs-down sign.'

Alicia and I both said 'Yeah' at the same time.

'That was the hardest scene for me,' Ritchie said, straight-faced.

'Why was that?' Alicia wanted to know.

4 **setting** a place sb or sth is in – 17 **pointer** used to point at things on the board – 21 **to snuggle up** to move up close to – 23 **catwalk** ['kætwɔ:k] a platform which models walk along to show the latest clothing fashions

I rolled my eyes at Ritchie. What he meant was obvious to me.

'You don't know?' he said to Alicia as if he couldn't believe it.

Alicia looked at me, then at Ritchie. 'Come on, tell me,' she said.

Ritchie laughed and said, 'Sarah will tell you why.'

I gave him a sharp look, then turned to Alicia. Her eyes were all over my face. 'Ritchie's joking. He means the scene was hard for him because it was hard for him to pretend he didn't like what he saw.'

Alicia thought about my answer for a moment, then smiled suddenly. 'What he saw – you mean us in our costumes coming down the catwalk?'

'Exactly.'

Alicia looked Ritchie in the eye, then turned to me. 'Maybe he wasn't joking,' she said.

'Maybe he wasn't,' Ritchie said.

Just then, the waitress who had served us came to our table and stood next to Ritchie. 'How were the pizzas?' she asked, giving him a playful look.

11 **to pretend** to act as if sth is true when you know that it is not

'Good!' Alicia said.

'Very good,' I said.

'Perfect,' Ritchie said, laughing.

'Can I get you something else?' the waitress said.

'I'll have another Coke,' Alicia said.

I shook my head. 'I'm okay,' I said.

'What about you?' she said, smiling into Ritchie's face.

'Could I have another coffee?' Ritchie said.

'Anything you want, big boy.' She winked at him again, then took our plates and hurried off.

'Have you posted the video on YouTube yet?' I asked Ritchie.

'Nope. It has to be edited first. Jerry said I could pick it up Monday afternoon.'

'I can't wait to see it,' Alicia said.

'I can't either,' I said. 'Let's hope they do a good job of editing it.'

'They will,' said Ritchie, nodding.

I shook my head. 'They'll have to. With something like 145 million videos on YouTube, it'll have to be quite special to get noticed.'

Ritchie gave a little laugh. 'It's got a lot going for it,' he said. 'First of all, there's the word 'love' in the title. That's always an attention getter.'

I nodded and said, 'What else?'

Ritchie smiled. 'Then there's the two of you in your hot costumes,' he said, winking at me. 'When guys see you, they'll click on the video, believe me.'

Ritchie and I laughed. Alicia was trying to smile, but her eyes weren't cooperating.

Full of hurt, they were fixed on mine.

14 **to edit** to examine and make corrections – 20 **something like** approximately; used to show that a description is not exact – 23 **a lot going for it** (having) many good qualities

6
Caught in the act

'Do you realize what you're doing? I thought you were my friend.'

These were Alicia's first words when we met for lunch break in the schoolyard. We always spend the first half hour of the break there, before going to the cafeteria. That way, we avoid the long food lines. Also, it gives us a better chance to talk privately than in the cafeteria. It was cold and windy outside, but the sun was shining. We began to walk.

I had been expecting her to say something like that. Still, I paused a moment, as if I couldn't understand what she was talking about. Finally, I let out a little laugh. 'You mean Ritchie and me? Hey, he was only flirting. He flirts with all the girls. You know Ritchie. That's just the way he is.'

Alicia gave me a sharp look. 'Yeah, that's the way Ritchie is, but what about you? I didn't think you were like that. I thought you had more respect for me. That was a serious, two-way flirt. Right in my face, for crap sake! Damn it, Sarah, were you trying to hurt me or something?'

I looked away, out across the schoolyard. I had to. I couldn't look Alicia in the eye. I felt like a robber caught in the act.

'Sarah? Hey!'

'No,' I began slowly, turning to face her. 'I certainly didn't want to hurt you. It – it just happened. I didn't plan it that way.'

22 **for crap sake** *sl, vulg* used to make clear that you are angry about sth – 25 **robber** sb who takes from sb or sth without permission – 26 **caught in the act** seen when doing sth wrong

'Didn't plan it that way? What about your makeup and that sexy costume?'

'Ritchie –', I began.

'Don't say Ritchie told us to wear a sexy costume. I know that. But that didn't mean you had to pick out a costume like you were going to the beach, for chrissake!'

I had that caught-in-the-act feeling again but tried not to show it. I decided to keep my mouth shut. Trying to defend myself would just make things worse. I only nodded.

We reached the end of the schoolyard and turned back. Alicia kept looking at me.

'Well?' she said finally.

I tried to look and sound as shocked as possible. 'What do you want me to say? That I've fallen for Ritchie? That I'm trying to steal him from you?'

Alicia stopped walking and looked me in the eye. 'That's it, exactly,' she said.

I shook my head. 'I just wanted to have some fun, that's all. You're overreacting!'

Alicia hesitated a moment, her eyes running up and down my face. At last she nodded and gave me a strange smile. Suddenly, a sad look came into her eyes. 'I hope you're telling the truth. Ritchie means a lot to me. You do, too.'

I didn't know what to say, but I knew I had to say something. 'I know, I know. Everything will be alright. You'll see,' I stammered, sounding like an actress who hadn't learned her lines well.

6 **for chrissake** ['kraɪseɪk] *inf* used to show that you are angry – 10 **to defend sb** to make sure sb is not hurt – 16 **to fall for sb** to fall in love with sb – 29 **to stammer** to speak with difficulty, often stopping – 30 **actress** ['æktrəs] a woman who plays roles in films or in the theater

We entered the school, went straight to our lockers and put away our jackets. After that, we hurried through the wide corridor and down the steps to the cafeteria. It was more crowded than usual, probably because it was so cold outside. Still, we were able to find a table where we could be by ourselves. I could see that Alicia wanted to continue the conversation we had in the schoolyard, but both of us knew it was better not to in the cafeteria, a room with a thousand ears. We continued talking but it was safe cafeteria talk. The private part of our conversation was over.

7
The power of positive thinking

I had to talk to Ritchie – alone! I had to find out where he stood – what his feelings were about me. But how? Without Alicia finding out? *Sarah, we have a problem!*

I thought about it all day Saturday. Then, when I was having supper I got a text message from Alicia saying she had to go to her grandfather's birthday with her parents tomorrow afternoon and couldn't come over as planned. I was disappointed at first, but quickly realized it was a lucky break. It gave me the chance to talk with Ritchie! Now all I had to do was contact him and get him to agree to meet me.

I thought for a moment, then got out my cell phone and texted, *can we meet 2moro pm?*

I didn't know what to do with myself while waiting for his answer. At first I just stared at my display but that soon got on my nerves so I went to my room and turned on the TV. After surfing through several channels, I found something interesting: the Miami Heat against the Boston Celtics. I was a big Celtics fan. They had won their last twelve games. Superstitious fans were afraid they would lose today, game number thirteen. Unlucky thirteen, you know? I wasn't superstitious. I was sure they'd beat Miami but was surprised when I saw the score: 106 to 95 at the end of the third quarter – Miami was in the lead!

11 **disappointed** unhappy because sth that you hoped for has not happened or not been as good as you expected *(enttäuscht)* – 12 **a lucky break** good luck – 24 **superstitious** [ˈsuːpɚstɪʃəs] believing that things can bring good or bad luck – 29 **in the lead** [liːd] at the front

But the fourth quarter began with 5 points in a row for Boston. I smiled. My guys are on the right track now, I thought. But as the game went on, Miami held on to their lead In fact, with only five minutes to go it had increased to ten points. I was growing nervous, but I was still sure the Celtics would turn it around. They'd often won games in the last minute. They were so good under pressure, especially Shaq. Then something happened that made me really nervous: my cell phone beeped. Holding my breath, I read the message: *meet u Mattapan Station 3 o'clock.*

The words seemed to reach out and grab my heart, taking my breath away. I sat very still and forced myself to breathe in slowly and deeply. After

1 **in a row** [roʊ] one after another – 2 **to be on the right track** thinking in the right way – 9 **Shaq** Shaquille O'Neil, Boston Celtics star player – 13 **to grab** to take suddenly – 15 **to breathe in** [bri:ð] to take in air

a while, a smile crossed my face. *Good work, Sarah!* I thought. *You did it. Tomorrow you get your heart-to-heart with Ritchie!*

A moment later, my smile was gone, replaced by a worried look. I had slipped into a crazy daydream. I was walking through the woods. Suddenly, I saw what looked like a cave. I went inside. At first, everything was covered in darkness. Then I heard a loud growl. Instead of running out of the cave, I went in deeper. All at once, I saw the form of something coming toward me. I turned to run but all I could see were high walls.

When I woke from my daydream, I was angry with myself for dreaming such stupid stuff. But the more I thought about it, the calmer I became. *You shouldn't be afraid of meeting Ritchie,* I said to myself. *You should be happy. Ritchie will be glad to see you. The two of you will have a good talk.* I repeated these words, over and over.

After a while, I began to feel better. The power of positive thinking had worked for me again.

When I turned to the TV, the game had just ended. Final score:130-128 for the Celtics! Positive thinking works for them, too, I thought.

2 **heart-to-heart** close, intimate, personal talk – 5 **to slip into** here: to suddenly start (having a daydream) – 9 **growl** [graʊl] a low, deep noise *(Knurren)*

8
Tour through Mattapan

The subway ride from South Station to Mattapan took about fifteen minutes. I sat thinking about being with Ritchie alone. I was growing more nervous by the minute. Suddenly, I heard the words, 'Next stop, Mattapan'. A moment later, the door opened and I hurried outside.

'Hi, Sarah!' were Ritchie's first words to me when I came out of the station. He gave me a quick hug. 'This is my home territory,' he said, laughing. 'Have you ever been here before?'

'Are you kidding?' I said. 'I'm a Boston girl. I grew up here.'

There was a playful look in Ritchie's eye. 'But nice Boston girls don't come to Mattapan. We've got a bad reputation.'

I knew that. I think most everyone in Boston knew that. Just a few weeks ago, Mattapan was once again in the headlines, 'Mass Murder in Mattapan!' This time, someone had shot and killed four people, including a two-year-old child, in broad daylight. That was an incident that shocked not only the city of Boston but the whole nation. I nodded slowly and said, 'I know. To be honest, I've only been here once. With a school class. We did a tour of Boston.'

'Including Mattapan? I'm surprised. Maybe the teacher wanted you to see the 'dark side' of Boston,' Ritchie said in a bitter tone of voice.

'Come on,' I said with a little laugh, 'it's not that bad here, is it?'

10 **hug** when you put your arms around sb and hold them tightly – 13 **to kid** *inf* to say sth that is not really true, as a joke – 22 **in broad daylight** *am helllichten Tag* – 23 **incident** [ˈɪntsɪdənt] a thing that happens – 25 **to be honest** [ˈɑːnɪst] what I really think is true *(um ganz ehrlich zu sein …)*

'Too true,' he said. 'There's more to Mattapan than what the media say about us. There's a good side to Mattapan that you don't hear so much about.'

I nodded and was about to say something when Ritchie suddenly smiled and said, 'I know you've come here to have a talk. We'll get to that, but – if you don't mind – I'd like to take you on a little tour first. My Mattapan. Is that all right?'

'Sure, okay, I don't mind.'

'Great, let's go!' Suddenly, he took me by the hand and we started off down the street. I was surprised by the large number of young men, mostly blacks and Latinos, I saw just standing around on the street corners in small groups. I was also surprised at how many of them nodded or shouted 'Hey, man' to Ritchie as we walked by. He seemed to be well known in Mattapan.

As we went on, I couldn't help but notice the large number of children playing in the streets. They seemed to be everywhere. Their happy faces were in sharp contrast to the dark looks of the young men.

We had been walking about a half hour when Ritchie suddenly stopped. He pointed to a convenience store. 'Here's where I work,' he said. 'Six days a week.'

My eyes opened wide. 'I didn't know you had a job.'

'You never asked me. Maybe you're surprised because I meet Alicia and you every day after school. Well, I've got the early shift. From 6 to 2 o'clock.'

6 **if you don't mind** a polite way to ask sb to do sth – 25 **convenience store** *(esp AE)* a store that sells food, newspapers, etc. and often stays open 24 hours a day – 31 **shift** the period of time when a person works, e.g. from 9 till 5.

'Oh, man. That *is* early. It must be hard getting up that early.'

'It is. But I need the job. We need the money. My mother's out of work. Been out of work ever since she got sick a couple of years ago.'

I gave him a sad look. 'I'm sorry to hear that. I – I didn't realize – '

'It's okay,' he said quickly. 'I don't talk about personal things a lot.'

'I can understand that,' I said.

Ritchie took my hand and we started walking again. After a while, he said, 'As I said, I don't usually talk so personally, but I want you to know these things. I want you to understand me better, and know why I am so serious about my rap career,' he said, looking me in the eye. 'Rapping's not just for fun, it's not just a hobby, it's very important to me because it's a way out.'

'A way out?'

'As I said, my mother's sick and out of work. She'd always been happy living here in Mattapan. She grew up here, she's got all her friends here. The apartment we live in is small but it's comfortable.' He paused, shaking his head. 'The problem is, things have changed.'

'What's changed?' I said quickly.

Ritchie thought for a moment, then began slowly. 'Mattapan's changed and my mother's changed,' he said. 'Mattapan has become a more dangerous place. There was always crime here, but it just keeps getting worse every year.' Ritchie shook his head.

18 **way out** a way to get away from a place you don't want to be in – 29 **dangerous** if sth is ~, it is likely to hurt you – 30 **crime** actions that are not legal

'That's a fact, it's not just what's in the headlines of the yellow press.'

'And your mother?'

'Yeah, she's changed, too. Her nerves are getting worse. She used to get out every day and talk with people. Now she stays inside a lot. She says it's getting to be too dangerous to be out on the street. She used to do all the shopping. Now she often asks me to get the food and stuff we need.'

'Is she afraid?'

Ritchie nodded. 'Yeah, she's afraid. The more she hears about all the crime that's going on here, the more she stays inside, and the more she stays inside, the more afraid she becomes. It's a vicious circle.'

We continued walking slowly down the street. As we approached another group of young men, one of them started staring at me. I felt like I was going through a full body scanner. His eyes were all over me. Then, just as we were passing them, he whistled at me. I drew in a deep breath as my heart started pounding. Ritchie tightened his hold on my hand. 'Ignore him,' he said.

We kept on walking. Ritchie stopped from time to time to show me places, like the outdoor basketball court where he often played and the grade school he had gone to. After a while, I turned to him and said, 'Leaving Mattapan wouldn't be easy for you, would it?'

Ritchie nodded slowly. 'Too true,' he said, 'I love this place, but I hate what it's doing to my mother.

2 **yellow press** the kind of newspaper, magazine, etc. that turns the news into sensational stories in order to sell more copies – 14 **vicious circle** when a problem creates a new problem that causes the original problem again *(Teufelskreis)* – 21 **to whistle** ['wɪsl] to make a sound by pushing air out through your lips – 22 **to pound** here: to beat quickly and loudly – 26 **court** [kɔːrt] a place where games such as tennis, basketball, etc. are played – 26 **grade school** *AE, inf* a school for children between the ages of approximately 6 and 12

I've got to try to get her out of here to a place where she can make a new start – before it's too late.' He shook his head. 'It's getting so she can't sleep at night. And – worst of all – she's starting to drink again. She denies it but I've seen the bottles. Damn it, Sarah, I don't want her to end up like my dad…'

I looked off and nodded.

'So now you know why I dropped out of school.'

'I – I understand.' I shook my head and gave a little laugh. 'And all the time I thought you – you'd got in some kind of trouble.'

'What kind of trouble?'

'Don't ask me. There were rumors at school. Kids were saying thing about you. You know – talking.'

Ritchie thought about it a moment. 'I guess I shouldn't be surprised at that.'

'That's the way it is in school.'

'School sucks, doesn't it?' he said, a sad look in his eye.

5 **to deny** to say that sth is not true – 8 **to drop out** *inf* to leave school too soon – 13 **rumor** ['ru:mɚ] a piece of information or a story which people talk about, which may or may not be true – 18 **to suck** *AE, sl* to be bad

9
No guarantees

We walked on and after a while he said, 'But what about you? You came here because you've got something on your mind you want to talk about. And here I've been talking about me the whole time.'

I let out a nervous little laugh. 'That's all right,' I said. I paused a moment to collect my thoughts, then began slowly. 'I've been thinking about the day at the studio. I can't get it out of my mind.'

Ritchie looked at me, expecting me to say more. When I didn't, he said, 'It was great fun, wasn't it?'

I studied his face. 'Yeah, great fun – and more.'

'More?'

'The way you looked at me.'

Ritchie stopped and took a step back. 'What way?'

'Come on, Ritchie, you know what I mean.' I studied his face some more, but it was like a mask. I couldn't get behind it. I was about to give up when he cracked a smile.

'You mean with eyes like these!' He looked at me with wide-open eyes and laughed.

I shook my head in surprise.

Ritchie stopped laughing and started walking again. After a while, he turned to me, a serious look on his face. 'Yeah, okay, I felt it, too. You're an attractive girl, you know. I was, well, like attracted to you.'

5 **on your mind** [maɪnd] if sth is ~, you think and worry about it a lot – 22 **to crack** to suddenly begin (to smile)

Smiling, I stepped up closer to him. 'Is that all?' I said, putting my hand on his shoulder.

He pulled his arm away as if my hand was red hot. Shocked, I stepped back. There was a stressed-out expression on his face. He looked me in the eye. 'Listen, Sarah,' he said. 'I'm in a very difficult situation at the moment. I don't have to spell it out to you, do I? There's Alicia – I still have strong feelings for her. I wouldn't want to hurt her. There's my mom and the whole problem with living here in Mattapan. And then there's the rap video, maybe my big chance to move away from here.' He paused. 'You understand, don't you?'

I thought a moment. 'You tell me. What is it I should understand?'

'Damn it, Sarah, you're not making this easy for me, you know that?' He shook his head.

I waited for him to continue.

'Okay, it's like this: I cannot – I repeat, I cannot at this time make any big decisions. I can't use any more stress than what I got right now. So it'd be good if you could just chill out for a while, put things on hold, if you get what I mean. I need time. I need room – to breathe. Otherwise, I – I don't know. It's – it's all just too much for me right now.' He got up close and looked me deep in the eye.

I knew what he wanted me to say, but I turned away. You know what they say about when you die – that your whole life – like a video – flashes before you? Well, right now I was having an experience like that. Within a few moments, several clear thoughts went through my mind.

3 **red hot** very hot – 5 **expression** the way your face looks when it shows feelings – 7 **to spell out** to explain the details of – 20 **to use** *inf* used to say you would like to have sth very much – 22 **to chill out** *inf* to relax and stop feeling angry or nervous about sth – 22 **to put on hold** to postpone, not do until later – 30 **experience** sth you have done or that has happened to you

Thought number one: Ritchie's chances of making a breakthrough and starting on a career as a rapper were definitely not good. There were so many excellent rappers in the scene and for every winner there were probably thousands of losers, kids who set their hearts on a rapping career but who didn't make it.

Thought number two: Even if he did make a breakthrough, what would my parents say about me going with a rapper? They wouldn't like it, that's for sure.

Thought number three (and the most important thought of all): What about Alicia? If Ritchie dropped Alicia for me, she'd be badly hurt and I would lose my best friend.

'Sarah?'

I turned back to Ritchie and was surprised to hear myself say, 'Okay, I'm willing to wait.'

He took me in his arms. 'Good, but you need to understand that I can't promise you anything, no happy-ending guarantees, in fact no guarantees at all. I'd like to be able to, but things are just too complicated. I don't know how things will turn out. I can't see into the future.' He gave me a sad little smile. 'No crystal ball – that's my problem.'

I took a deep breath. 'I don't have one, either,' I said.

'So for the time being, we'll just go along as if everything is cool – me, Alicia and you, all right?' he said.

'Yeah, you, me and Alicia,' I said, trying to smile.

2 **breakthrough** ['breɪkθruː] a person's first important success – 6 **to set your heart on** to want very much – 10 **to go with sb** *inf* to have sb as a boyfriend or girlfriend – 14 **to drop sb** *inf* to stop going with sb – 25 **crystal ball** ['krɪstl] a ball made of glass used by people who say they can tell the future by looking into it

We started walking again. The neighborhood we were now approaching looked even more run-down than the ones we'd gone through. After some time, Ritchie suddenly turned to me and said, 'Last stop on my tour. You see that building over there?' He pointed at a small apartment building on the other side of the street. 'On the third floor – that's where I live!'

I nodded but didn't say anything. What could you say about a building like that?

'I know what you're thinking,' he said. 'I know – it doesn't look like much on the outside, but the apartments are nice.'

'I'm sure they are,' I said.

'You're probably wondering why I'm showing it to you. Well, I want you to know where I come from. So you can understand me better.'

I nodded slowly. I was expecting him to ask me if I wanted to meet his mother. I was surprised when he didn't.

On the subway ride home, I had a lot to think about. So much that I almost missed my stop.

2 **run-down** a ~ building is a building that is falling to pieces – 15 **to wonder** [ˈwʌndɚ] to ask yourself

10
Ritchie's new rap

When Alicia and I met Ritchie after school on Monday, he was smiling all over his face. 'I just had a look at YouTube,' he said.

'And – are we getting lots of clicks?' I said.

'Yeah, we are. Over five hundred already. That's very good in such a short time,' Ritchie said.

We gave each other high fives and began walking slowly towards the school parking lot and Alicia's car.

Alicia laughed. 'Some of the kids in class told me they had seen it. They congratulated me. They said it was really good.'

'The same thing happened to me,' I said, smiling.

Ritchie nodded. 'I got some compliments, too, but I also got some good advice from Jerry about the video.'

'What kind of advice?' I wanted to know.

'He said a lot of musicians, once they produce a video, make the mistake of sitting around, counting clicks on YouTube, and waiting for something to happen. That's not good for your creativity, he said. His advice was to ignore YouTube and continue to focus on making music. Not to stop.'

We reached Alicia's car and got in. I was still thinking about Jerry's advice when Alicia turned to Ritchie and said, 'I'm sure Jerry knows what he's talking about. I agree. You should continue writing your raps. Who knows? Maybe some day, when we earn our first million, we could get them

10 **parking lot** *AE* a place where people can leave their cars – 17 **advice** when you tell sb what they could or should do in a situation

all produced. Then Sarah and I could be rap babes again.' Laughing, she started the car and pulled slowly out of her parking space.

'I've been doing some thinking,' Ritchie said, suddenly serious. 'I was thinking about our day at the studio. We learned a lot that day, didn't we?'

'I certainly did!' I said quickly.

'Me, too,' Alicia said, nodding. She drove through the parking lot exit and turned into the street.

'Maybe we learned enough to produce our own videos. What do you guys think?' Ritchie said, laughing.

'No question about it,' I said.

'All we need is a video camera,' Ritchie said with a little laugh.

'No problem,' I said quickly. 'We've got one at home.'

'Hey! We'll be our own video production company!' said Alicia.

'Not so fast, dude,' I said. 'Ritchie's got to write a new rap first.'

Ritchie turned in his seat and looked at me. 'Wrong, dude. Ritchie's already written a new one.'

'You got it with you?' I wanted to know.

'Right here,' he said, smiling and pointing at his pocket.

'Well, let's hear it,' said Alicia.

Ritchie made a stop sign with his hand. 'Not so fast!' he said. 'I need a cup of coffee first.'

'You and your coffee,' I said playfully. 'How many cups of coffee do you drink a day, anyway?'

'A few,' Ritchie said in a flat voice.

1 **rap babe** *inf* a girl who takes part in a rap video, e.g. as a dancer – 20 **dude** [du:d] *sl* a name which you give a friend: 'Hi, ~ !' – 31 **anyway** Alicia uses this word to emphasise what she says

'A few?' I said. Alicia and I laughed at the same time.

'It's a habit,' he said. 'Maybe not a good habit, but it's better than other habits I can think of.'

For a long moment no one spoke. Finally, Alicia gave a little laugh and said, 'Can you hold on a little longer? There's a Starbucks just down the road from here.'

'Thank God!' Ritchie said, straight-faced.

A moment later, we drove into the Starbucks parking lot. It was a busy time of day, the restaurant was full. Standing in line, we had lots of time to choose from the menu.

After we got our coffee and found a table, Ritchie pulled out a piece of paper. 'Are you ready for this?' He grinned.

Alicia and I grinned back. 'Ready!' we said.

'The name of this rap is "Mattapan",' he said. He leaned forward and started rapping out a beat on the table. He closed his eyes a moment. When he opened them, he began reading.

Mattapan's bleeding,
bleeding, bleeding,
streets full of blood.
Drug wars, drug lords,
guns everywhere,
gunshots in the night,
rat-a-tat-tat, rat-a-tat-tat,
shattering sleep,
shattering hopes
of peace in Mattapan.

19 **to lean** to move the upper part of your body – 25 **lord** a very important man – 29 **to shatter** to make sth end – 31 **peace** a situation in which there is no war *(Frieden)*

Gangs roam the streets
of Mattapan,
their territory,
kings of the jungle,
law of the jungle,
red in tooth and claw,
only the strongest survive,
no mercy,
kids killing kids,
shocking the community.

Ritchie looked up and said, ‘Here comes the refrain.’

Mattapan, Mattapan,
a bad scene, man.
A sick scene,
deadly ill,
violence growing
like cancer
in Mattapan.

Ritchie repeated the refrain, then paused a moment. ‘Now for the second verse,’ he said.

The people of Mattapan
aren’t blind,
they see, they hear,
they know who they are,
the murderers
of Mattapan,

1 **to roam** to go around a place without knowing where you’re going – 5 **law of the jungle** a situation in which people are prepared to harm other people in order to get what they want – 6 **red in tooth and claw** *coll* used to say that in the jungle animals live by killing other animals – 8 **mercy** [ˈmɜːsi] *Gnade* – 10 **community** all the people who live in a town, city, etc. – 17 **violence** *Gewalt* – 18 **cancer** a serious illness *(Krebs)* – 26 **murderer** [ˈmɜːdərər] a person who has killed sb deliberately and illegally

but paralysed by shock
and fear
they stand by helplessly.
They love their community
but have learned
the hard way:
if you wanna stay alive
in Mattapan,
keep your mouth shut, man,
‘cause talkin’ to the cops
will get you shot
in Mattapan.
Just be cool, man,
don’t be a fool, man,
don’t play the hero,
the cool survive,
heroes die
in Mattapan.

After a short pause, Ritchie ended the rap by repeating the refrain three or four times, softer each time.

Smiling, he took a long drink of his caffè latte. ‘Well? How did you like it?’ He looked first at Alicia, then at me.

Alicia shook her head. ‘Isn’t it kind of, uh, dark?’

‘Dark? What do you mean dark?’ Ritchie wanted to know.

‘Dark. You know – negative, without hope. Is it really that bad?’

Ritchie thought a moment, then said. ‘When you love something you always want it to be better. That’s why you criticize.’

1 **paralysed** unable to move – 6 **the hard way** by having bad or difficult experiences – 11 **to get you shot** *inf* to get yourself hurt or killed by gunfire – 14 **fool** a silly person – 25 **kind of** used to show that what you are saying is not exact

I smiled to myself. *Wow! That's Ritchie the deep thinker again.*

'Besides,' he went on, 'Raps are almost always negative. That's the rap mode. Raps aren't like love songs.'

'What the rap says about Mattapan is not that wrong,' I blurted out.

Alicia gave me a sharp look. 'How do you know?' she said. 'Have you been there?'

'When I was in middle school – with a class. We did a tour of Boston. Our teacher took us to Mattapan.' I felt my face growing warm. 'I'll never forget it,' I said, shaking my head. 'We were scared the whole time.'

Alicia's sharp look slowly softened. 'I guess it is bad there,' she said. 'At least that's what they say on television.'

I nodded and smiled but inside I was kicking myself for being so stupid. Not knowing what to say, I got busy spooning whipped cream from my Mocha into my mouth.

'Sometimes the stuff in the media is exaggerated,' Ritchie said. 'But they get it right most of the time.'

Alicia and I nodded. Alicia took a long drink of her Carmel Macchiato, and I spooned some more whipped cream into my mouth.

'Well?' Ritchie was watching us, amused. 'What about the video production? You guys got any ideas?'

For the next half hour or so, we talked about possible scenes for the video. It was a lively discussion. Knowing that Alicia was watching me

7 **to blurt out** to say sth suddenly and without thinking about it carefully enough – 18 **to kick yourself** *inf* to be angry with yourself because you have done something silly – 20 **whipped cream** cream in solid form – 22 **to exaggerate** [ɪɡˈzædʒəreit] to make the thing you are talking about bigger, better or worse than it actually is

and Ritchie very closely, I continued to be careful not to show my new-found feelings for him. He seemed to be thinking the same thing. He was his usual charming self, especially charming to Alicia.

11
Homemade video

That Saturday, we – Ritchie and his boys, Alicia and me – worked at producing the new video. We were in the party room at Alicia's place.

Ritchie had come well prepared. He had a copy of the production plan for each of us. He also brought along a tape with the pre-recorded background music. He had chosen a slow, heavy beat, just right for the dark mood of the rap. And he had brought along a friend – Russell was his name – to help with the filming.

In the first scene we mimed a kind of gang war, each of us armed with toy guns. It was like a scene from one of those shoot-'em-up computer games. Alicia and I were the Eagles, Rico, Jackson and Scooter the Bloodsuckers. Rico and Jackson were laughing wildly and making loud shooting noises at first. But as soon as Ritchie was ready to begin, everyone got serious. The 'war' was a kind of dance, and the choreography to it was well planned, every step of it.

Walking around like dressed up in a hoody and baggy pants was huge fun.

I mean, when do you as a girl get the chance to play a macho role? Walking like a boy walks, talking like a boy talks – it was a whole new experience.

Ritchie had told Alicia and me to try to look as aggressive and angry as possible. I tried but every time I looked at Alicia I had to laugh. Like me, she was wearing a hoody and baggy pants. What a

10 **mood** the way you are feeling at the moment – 23 **hoody** *sl* a sweatshirt with a part (called the hood) that can be pulled over your head – 24 **baggy pants** loose-fitting trousers

sight! The first few times I started laughing it was funny and everyone laughed, too, but after a while it wasn't funny any longer. Ritchie told me to pull myself together. We'd never get finished, he said, if things went on that way.

When the 'gang war' was over, we all lay on the floor wounded or dead, while Ritchie rapped the refrain: 'Mattapan, Mattapan, a bad scene, man, a sick scene, deadly ill…'

For the next scene, the one for the second verse, we changed roles. Alicia and me, Rico and Scooter were now residents of Mattapan, Jackson played the part of the cop.

In this scene we, the 'residents', didn't have much to do, just stand around and look frightened. When the 'cop' went by, we turned to him as if we wanted to tell him something, but suddenly stopped and stood still. We were 'paralyzed by fear' as the rap put it.

Finally, Ritchie rapped the refrain at the end, and we sank to the floor and lay there without moving. Then Russell said 'Cut!' for the last time and we jumped up, laughing and exchanging high fives.

The hours we spent making the video were happy hours, full of action and fun. But there was a serious side to it, too. At the level of body language, there had been a whole lot of serious interaction going on, Alicia interacting with me, Alicia with Ritchie, and Ritchie with me.

Alicia was watching my body language, especially my interaction with Ritchie. I could feel her eyes on me. Every smile, every roll of the eyes – she didn't

3 **to pull yourself together** to take control of your feelings – 7 **wounded** [wu:ndɪd] hurt by an object such as a knife, gun, bomb, etc. – 12 **resident** the people who live in a certain house or a city *(Einwohner)* – 23 **to exchange** if people ~ things, they give them to each other at the same time

miss a thing. I had to be careful. Ritchie wanted it that way. He had been very clear about that.

Of course, I was watching Alicia and Ritchie, too. And, to my surprise, it seemed as if nothing had changed between them. As if nothing had happened between Ritchie and me. I couldn't believe what a good actor he was!

12
Alicia freaks out

A few days after the making of the video, Alicia was at my place. She needed help, she said, with an assignment for Spanish. I doubted that that was the real reason for her coming over, and when she showed me the text she needed help with, I was sure that she could have done the work herself. But I played along, waiting to see what was on her mind.

It wasn't long before I found out. We finished the assignment quickly. I made us a pot of tea – the perfect drink on a cold November evening – and Alicia soon got into a talking mood.

Alicia was holding her cup in both hands, looking at me intently. 'Ritchie has changed,' she said suddenly.

'Changed?'

'Yeah, he's not, uh, warm like he was. You know what I mean.' She gave a nervous little laugh, her eyes fixed on mine.

I nodded slowly, waiting for her to continue. When she didn't, I said, 'Have you talked with him about it?'

'Not yet. I wanted to talk to you first.'

I realized I was in a minefield. I spoke slowly, choosing my words carefully. 'I've got the feeling that Ritchie is under a lot of pressure. I'm not sure why, but maybe it's got to do with this whole rap business. He seems to be very nervous about it.'

5 **assignment** a piece of work you are given to do – 5 **to doubt** [daʊt] to think it is probably not true or possible – 9 **to play along** to act as if you agree – 26 **minefield** *here*: a situation in which there are hidden dangers and difficulties – 28 **to be under pressure** to have the feeling that you have a lot to do but too little time to do it in – 30 **business** [ˈbɪznɪs] here: used in a general way to mean the thing you are talking about

Alicia nodded, but didn't say anything.

I took a drink of my tea while trying to find the right words. 'Maybe he's so nervous because he needs money. Maybe he's in some kind of financial trouble.'

'I never thought of it that way. He does come from a poor part of town, doesn't he? Maybe you're right about that. Maybe he does need money.'

Relieved that Alicia seemed to agree with me, I gave her a sad smile. 'Could be. To us, being rap babes is just fun. We don't do it because of the money, do we?'

Alicia shook her head. 'Not really,' she said. She thought a moment, then said, 'That would explain why he's acting so – so strange now.'

I nodded, giving her my warmest motherly smile.

After a while, she put her hand on mine. 'I feel better now,' she said. 'I knew it would help to talk with you about this.'

The right moment had come to change the topic. I refilled my cup with tea, took a long drink and leaned back in my chair. 'You remember Ritchie asking us to try to come up with a rap of our own? Did you try?'

'Uh, no, not really. I haven't had the time. Have you?'

'Yep.' I let out a nervous laugh. 'When I first sat down to write it, I thought it would be easy. An hour later, I gave up. I'd only written five lines. But when I went back to it the next day, everything seemed to fall into place.' Noticing the unhappy look on Alicia's face, I added quickly, 'Everything except the

9 **relieved** feeling happy because sth bad has not happened or is no longer happening – 20 **topic** a subject that you talk, learn or write about – 32 **except** *außer*

ending. I'm not satisfied with the ending. Perhaps you can help me with it.'

Silence. Alicia eyed me suspiciously.

I forced a little smile. 'Do you want to hear it?' I said nervously.

She hesitated.

'Well?' I said.

'Okay,' she said in a flat tone.

I went over to my desk and looked through the stuff on top of it until I found the piece of paper I was looking for, then went back to where I had been sitting.

'It's about Boston,' I said. 'I call it The Heart of Boston Rap.'

Alicia nodded.

I smiled at her but she didn't smile back. Then, nervously, I began to rap.

I hate the crap
that's happening
in my town,
Boston.
Everyone says, Boston,
awesome, perfect city,
picture postcard pretty,
oooohhh,
with sooo much history,
Boston Tea Party,
Battle of Bunker Hill,
Paul Revere's ride:
'Listen my children
and you shall hear
of the midnight ride

1 **satisfied** happy because you got what you wanted – 3 **suspiciously** [səsˈpɪʃəsli] in a way that you show that you think sb has done sth wrong *(argwöhnisch)* – 18 **crap** *sl* stupid, untrue things – 23 **awesome** [ˈɑːsəm] causing a feeling of great respect for sth, because it is very good, large, etc.

of Paul Revere.'
Tourists love that stuff,
eat it up,
they don't realize
what natives know:
Boston's no big city.
Cosmopolitan?
No, man,
Boston's nothing but a big town,
closed down,
the heart of Boston
is cold,
not warm and friendly,
a stuffy town,
night life there is none,
sidewalks rolled up at ten.
University town,
they say,
Harvard, Cambridge
and MIT!
Hooray!
They don't say:
the students live in their own little world,
the campus is their home,
they're not really part of
Boston town.

I looked up at Alicia. She took a last long drink of her tea and put the empty cup on the table in front of her. She had a thoughtful look on her face.

Smiling, I asked if she wanted some more tea. When she nodded, I poured her another cup.

3 **eat sth up** *inf* to like sth so much you want to see or hear more – 5 **native** sb who has lived in a particular area, city or country all their life – 10 **closed down** *here*: not lively, not much going on – 14 **stuffy** boring, old-fashioned – 16 **to roll up the sidewalks** *AE* the streets are empty, nobody is out (sidewalk *AE* = *Bürgersteig*) – 20 **MIT** Massachusetts Institute of Technology

'Of course, it's a lot like Ritchie's Mattapan rap,' she said, fixing her eyes on mine.

'Yeah, you're right. I hadn't thought about that,' I said, laughing nervously.

'What about the ending? You said you weren't happy with it.'

'Right. And I was hoping you could help me with it.'

'Maybe I can,' she said. 'What's it about?'

'It's about racism.'

'Racism? Here in Boston?' she said. 'You must be joking.'

I shook my head. 'It's no joke. Racism is a big problem. Maybe not so much in the part of Boston we live in. But even here you hear some shocking racist remarks sometimes.'

Alicia thought about it, then nodded. 'Maybe you're right.'

'Tourists seem to think Boston's just one big happy family,' I said. 'But there are many parts of Boston they don't see. What they don't see is that Boston is basically a segregated city.'

Alicia gave me a questioning look. 'Hmm. Go ahead. Read me the rest,' she said.

I smiled at her as warmly as I could and began.

Integration?
In Boston?
Tourists say
Boston's one big happy family.
Little do they know,
that's not so,
no, no, no, no,

10 **racism** ['reɪsɪzm] a way of thinking that shows you believe that your race is better than others – 12 **to joke** to say sth in order to make people laugh – 16 **remark** [rɪ'mɑːrk] a few words that give the facts or your opinon about sb or sth – 22 **basically** used for saying that you are talking about the most important aspects of sth – 22 **segregated** separated according to race or religion

we're no UNO,
united nations,
we're divided nations,
living side by side,
not together.
Little Italy,
Chinatown,
Latino,
Irish,
Jewish,
Asian neighborhoods,
black ghettos,
we got it all,
even the WASPs
got their nests.
A melting pot Boston's not,
it's a salad bowl,
not a melting pot,
got it?
A salad bowl,
not a melting pot!

I looked at Alicia nervously.

She nodded slowly but said nothing. She seemed to be thinking.

'Well? That was the ending. What do you think?'

Suddenly, there was a flash of anger in her eyes. 'That's not the Boston I know. My God, you've made everything look so – so negative! Just like Ritchie!'

Shocked, I couldn't say anything. I just sat there looking at her.

Red in the face and in a loud voice, she said, 'It's not your Boston either! I know you like Boston

3 **divided** if a group is ~, there are serious disagreements among the people in the group – 14 **WASP** *abb* White Anglo-Saxon Protestant – 16 **melting pot** a situation in which there are many different types of people, ideas, religions, etc. existing together

just as much as I do. But you're trying to suck up to Ritchie. You think he'll like all that negative stuff. That's it, isn't it?'

I took a deep breath and looked Alicia in the eye. 'What's gotten into you? It's not like you to freak out like this.'

She got up suddenly and stood in front of me. 'You know what it is! Don't pretend you don't!'

I took another deep breath and said, 'If you sit down again we can talk about this. I'm not going to talk to you with you standing over me like this like – like a damn judge or something.'

Alicia glared at me a moment, then sat down. 'Well?' she said. 'I'm listening.'

I hesitated, searching for the right words. I picked up my cup and turned it slowly in my hands. I could feel Alicia's eyes staring at me as she waited for my answer.

'Well?' she said again.

'You're right about my rap. It is very much like Ritchie's, but I didn't copy his style intentionally. It just turned out that way. You're also right that I want him to like it.' I hesitated again and looked her in the eye. 'Is that so wrong?'

She said nothing at first as she studied my face. 'Maybe, maybe not. It all depends…' she said finally. Then she got up quickly and started for the door.

'Hey,' I said, 'what's your big hurry?'

'Got to get back,' she said.

'Aren't you going to help me with the ending?'

Alicia let out a loud laugh. 'Forget it. I'm sure Ritchie will like it as it is.'

1 **to suck up to** *sl* to be very nice to sb so that they will treat you well – 12 **judge** sb whose job it is to decide what is right or wrong *(Richter)* – 26 **It all depends** used when you cannot give a clear answer because different things are possible *(„kommt drauf an")*

13
See you at the gig!

Alicia stayed clear of me the next few days. That was hard on me. I missed her. But in the end I understood that she needed to be alone with her feelings. All I could do was wait and hope that we'd be back together again soon.

Of course, the fact that she continued to meet with Ritchie after school – but without me now – was *also* hard on me. I missed him, too, and kept asking myself did he miss me as much as I missed him?

Finally, on the fourth day (I counted them!) after our little fight, things suddenly changed. I was having lunch in the cafeteria and watching Alicia, two tables away, out of the corner of my eye. She was with a small group of girls from her class. They were talking loud and laughing. Alicia seemed to be laughing the loudest. *Is she putting on a show for me? Trying to demonstrate that she can get along*

3 **to stay clear of** not to get close to, keep away from – 20 **to demonstrate** to show clearly that sth is true or that it exists

very well without me? Damn it! She doesn't expect me to make the first move, does she? Suddenly, as if in answer to my question, she got up, came over to my table and sat down opposite me! Several heads turned in our direction. For a long moment, we didn't say much. We were like boxers at the start of a fight, eyeing each other, waiting to see what the other would do.

All at once, she leaned across to me. 'I wouldn't be here,' she said softly, 'but Ritchie asked me to talk to you.'

Ouch! That hurt! 'What about?' I said in a flat voice.

'It's about a gig!'

Poker-faced, I nodded. 'Yeah?' I said.

Her eyes were locked on mine. 'He wants you to join us.' She emphasized the word 'us'.

'Tell me more,' I said, trying not to show my excitement. I lowered my head and pretended I was concentrating on my lasagna.

'It's at the Roxbury Youth Club Center, on Saturday. We're part of a four-band program. Each band gets to perform a half hour.'

I nodded. 'And when is it our turn, do you know?'

'We're third.'

'Uh, huh.'

'Ritchie said third is good because the audience is mostly in a good mood by then,' she said with a little smile. Quoting Ritchie seemed to make her feel good.

'That's logical,' I said flatly.

All at once, she reached into her pocket and pulled out an envelope. 'I almost forgot. Here. This is for you. It's from Ritchie.'

14 **gig** *sl* a onetime job, *esp* music concert – 16 **to lock on** here: to look directly at sb for a long time – 29 **to quote** [kwoʊt] to say or write words that sb else has said or written – 33 **envelope** ['envəloʊp] a flat paper case to send letters in *(Umschlag)* –

'What is it?'

She gave a little laugh. 'Ritchie says it's your homework.' She paused a moment. 'He's picking us up at my place at 9 o'clock.'

I nodded and smiled at her. 'I'll be there,' I said, hoping to hear her say 'Great!' and 'I'll meet you after school', but instead she got up to go. 'Got to be off' and 'See you Saturday' was all she said.

I watched her go. For the next several minutes, I sat very still. The cafeteria, which was crowded and noisy a moment ago, now seemed strangely empty and quiet. My lasagna was growing cold but I didn't care. I had a lot to think about. At first, I thought about Alicia and the way she was treating me. I could understand that. She was jealous. If I were in her situation, I would probably act the same way. But then my thoughts turned to Ritchie. Ritchie wanted me back! I smiled as a warm feeling filled my whole body.

Suddenly, realizing I was holding Ritchie's envelope, I opened it quickly and pulled out two typewritten sheets of paper. On one was a rap, on the other notes for the performance of the rap – plus a P.S. in Ritchie's handwriting!

P.S. Hey, Sarah! Loved your rap about Boston. You've got talent, dude. See you at the gig Saturday. Ritchie

Suddenly, the cafeteria was noisy again, full of loud talk and laughter. I began to laugh, too.

13 **to care** to be interested in sth and feel strongly that it is important – 15 **jealous** feeling angry towards sb who has sth you would like to have *(eifersüchtig)*

14
A fantastic concert

We were lucky. A popular local band got the concert off to a good start. Then came the next band, Silver Mountain, a country, rock and blues band. They were just the right band for us. They were good but not too good. They were good enough to please the crowd, but not so good that the band following them would be doomed to failure. They were really cool, too, wishing us good luck as they cleared away their equipment to make room for us.

As soon as they finished, we got busy setting up our own equipment. A few minutes before, behind the stage, I'd been so nervous my hands were shaking. For a moment, I thought I was going to freak out. It didn't help that Alicia still wasn't speaking to me. She talked with Ritchie the whole time and didn't even look my way.

But now, on the stage, looking out at the large crowd, all that negative stuff was forgotten. All I felt now was a wonderful sense of excitement. *Let the show begin!* I thought.

A few moments later, spotlights came on and Ritchie ran onto the stage and waved to the crowd. Wearing a black bandana, a bright yellow T-shirt and matching wristbands, he looked great! I wasn't the only one who thought so. The girls in the front row were screaming and reaching out to him. Ritchie seemed to enjoy this. When he moved over close and gave them high fives, they screamed even louder. But when he raised his arm suddenly, the crowd quieted down quickly. I was impressed.

9 **doomed** [du:md] certain not to be successful – 9 **failure** *opp* of success – 16 **to freak out** *inf* to lose control of yourself – 26 **wristband** *Armband*

Other performers had to work hard to get their audience's attention. Not Ritchie.

He began by introducing each of us in the band. When he said my name, I smiled and made a victory sign. My heart was drumming with excitement.

After that, he looked around at the hundreds of faces. He knew exactly what he was doing. They were waiting for him to say something, but he was taking his time, not hurrying. Then, when the room was unbelievably quiet, he stepped up to the microphone. 'Our first rap is a kind of state of the union thing, some thoughts about the land I love, the land that makes me sad.' Then he smiled and added, 'It's kind of heavy. I hope you're in a serious listening mood.'

Just then, someone at the back shouted, 'Lay it on us, man!' and the crowd laughed.

Ritchie gave a nod of his head to Jackson on the drums. With a huge grin on his face, Jackson picked up his sticks and started laying down a slow, heavy beat. After that, Rico and Scooter joined in. Ritchie listened for a moment, then took the microphone in his hands and seemed to rest his head on it. After a while, he looked up sadly and started rapping.

Quo vadis, U.S.A.?
Where you goin'
America?
I'm proud of my country
but now I fear
she's lost her way
in the bushes of war.

4 **victory sign** a sign made with the fingers to form the letter 'v' for victory ("We will win!") – 11 **state of the union** a reference to the annual ~ speech given by the U.S. president about the condition the country is in – 14 **heavy** *sl* serious, deep – 16 **to lay it on sb** *sl* to say what you want to say – 20 **to lay down** *inf* to do, produce – 25 **quo vadis** *Lat* where are you going? – 28 **proud** *stolz*

War, war,
everywhere.
Is war the answer?
No, no,
a thousand times no.
We were blind,
believed the lies:
link with El Kaida
weapons of mass destruction,
pushed into a war
costing
thousands of lives,
billions of dollars,
a shameful war,
a crying shame,
a tragedy!
What about that more important war,
for hearts and souls,
for leadership in the world?
On your mark, get set, go!
The race is on,
and the winner is?
It's too soon to say,
but it don't look okay
for America.
In education
our youth,
the future of our nation,
have fallen far behind
the Asians.
Hong Kong,
China,

9 **weapons of mass destruction** weapons that can cause great damage to large areas – 14 **shameful** so bad that you feel sad and disappointed about it – 15 **a crying shame** used for underlining how bad or unfair sth is – 19 **leadership** the position of being more successful than those you are competing against – 20 **on your mark, get set, go**! sth called out to runners at the beginning of a race – 27 **youth** [ju:θ] young people

Singapore,
South Korea,
education's a passion
in Asia.
To us learning's boring,
our passion's sports
and shopping,
success counts
and money,
money, money, money,
the more the better,
just go and get it.
We laugh at intellectuals,
professors are cartoon characters,
our role models are movie stars,
home run hitters,
and last not least
Lady Gaga.
Have we gone gaga?
Quo vadis, U.S.A.?
Where you goin',
America?

When Ritchie finished, there was a moment of thoughtful silence, then applause and shouts of approval.

As for me, I was pleased with my performance. Having missed the final practice session, I was worried about how I would do. But I had managed to learn my part well. I had practiced on my own until I could do the choreography perfectly.

3 **passion** [ˈpæʃən] a very strong feeling – 15 **role model** sb who is seen as a good example to copy – 16 **home run hitter** a baseball player who scores a lot of points by hitting the ball so far that he can go around all four bases and score a run – 25 **approval** [əˈpruːvl] a good opinion of sb or sth – 27 **session** a period of time that is used to do a particular activity

As the crowd continued to applaud, Ritchie stood leaning on the microphone. Finally, when the crowd quieted down, he looked out at the audience and said, 'Our next number is called The Heart of Boston Rap.'

My rap! We're going to do my rap! Smiling, I looked around at Alicia but she was looking at Ritchie. I felt so proud. It would have made me even prouder, of course, if Ritchie had told the audience it was my rap, but he only winked at me. Okay, I thought, he's the one who has to rap it, not me.

During the rap, I looked out at the kids in the audience. I could see from their faces that not all of them agreed with my hard words about Boston, some of them were shaking their heads, others were even giving us the thumbs-down sign, but when it was over most of them were applauding. Smiling, Ritchie came over to me and squeezed my hand. When he returned to center stage, I glanced at Alicia. She was staring at me. *If looks could kill…*

When Ritchie announced the name of the next number, the Mattapan Rap, the crowd suddenly went quiet. Many of the kids were from Mattapan, the others all knew about Mattapan or 'murdapan' as it was called. All throughout the rap, the crowd remained quiet, listening closely to the lyrics. Ritchie was rapping about a place they all knew. When he finished, there were a few seconds of silence, but then a huge burst of applause.

At last, it was time for the final song. When Ritchie said it was about love, there were lots of oohs and aahs from the audience. Ritchie laughed, but

18 **to squeeze** to press together the parts of sth – 24 **'murdapan'** a new word made from 'murder' and 'Mattapan' to show how high the murder rate is in Mattapan – 26 **lyrics** the words of a song

quickly turned serious. 'Sorry,' he said, 'it's not *that* kind of love song. It's about the meaning of love.'

That got a huge 'ohhhhh!' and a lot of laughter from the crowd. Except, I noticed, for several girls in the front row. They weren't laughing. On the contrary, they were nodding their heads at Ritchie, wanting him to begin. One of them, a head-turning blonde, was staring at him with dreamy eyes – and Ritchie was staring back!

Ritchie waited for the crowd to settle down, then gave the band the start signal. During the rap I studied the faces in the crowd. Many of the kids were frowning, trying to understand what Ritchie was saying. But as he went on, their faces brightened as the meaning of the rap became clearer.

Finally, when he came to the refrain at the end, he asked the crowd to join in. And they did. Uncertainly the first time around, but by the third or fourth time, they were rapping like crazy, loud and clear.

As soon as it was over, the crowd went wild. Ritchie nodded to us and we all put our hands together and bowed as the audience continued to applaud. A warm bright feeling filled me as I stood there beside the others. Now I could understand why some performers risked their life diving into the audience at the end of a show. When you feel so much love, you're not afraid of anything.

We stood there for a long moment, smiling and bowing, our moment of glory. At the end of that moment, Ritchie said, 'Go!' We knew exactly what

10 **to settle down** to become quiet – 13 **to frown** to make a face that shows that you don't like sb or sth – 18 **to join in** to become part of sth – 24 **to bow** [baʊ] to move the upper part of your body forward – 27 **to dive** to suddenly jump toward sth that is on or near the ground

we had to do. Ritchie had told us how important it was to take down our equipment in time for the next act and put it away safely. We only had about ten minutes so we had to work fast.

We loaded the equipment in Scooter's old van, which was parked in a corner of the parking lot, directly opposite the side-door exit. When the last piece of equipment was inside, Scooter locked the van and we hurried back inside to watch the final act.

Dire Straits Recovered was an excellent cover band. Like me, most of the kids in the audience didn't know much about Dire Straits. They were long before our time. But already after a few beats of the first song, 'Walk of Life', the crowd was in a happy mood, nodding their heads and tapping their feet. After that, the band did 'Sultans of Swing' and the mood got even better. For their final song, the moving hymn 'Brothers in Arms', the lights were turned down low. The audience, some of them holding lighters, waved their arms rhythmically to the music. It was a perfect finale. There were tears in my eyes at the end.

7 **exit** sth that is used to go out of a place (e.g. a door) – 11 **recovered** [ˌriːˈkʌvɚd] a play on words: 'cover' as in 'cover version' and 'recovered' meaning 'brought back' – 16 **to tap** to lightly hit your fingers, feet, etc. against sth – 19 **moving** causing strong feelings – 21 **lighter** *Feuerzeug* – 22 **tear** [tɪr] when you cry, ~s come from your eyes *(Träne)*

15
Where's Ritchie?

Ritchie had said we would celebrate our first gig by going to the Madhatter, one of Boston's top discos. I was looking forward to that. Alicia and the others were, too. But suddenly, when the lights were turned back on, Alicia looked around and said, 'Where's Ritchie?' He'd been standing beside her and the others a few minutes ago. Where'd he go?

We stood there waiting at first, thinking he'd be back in a moment. But as the minutes went by and he didn't show up we decided to start looking for him.

'This won't be easy,' Rico said, looking around. The club room was still crowded.

Scooter shook his head. 'He can't be far. Our best chance is to split up. Alicia, you go along this side,' he said, pointing toward the left side. 'You, Sarah, go around the other side.'

'What about me?' Rico asked.

'You come with me,' Scooter said. 'We'll go through the middle.'

'And I'll go to the men's room,' said Jackson.

Scooter laughed. 'Good idea. Maybe he got caught in a traffic jam there.'

I looked at Scooter. 'Wait a minute. Where do we meet? Back here?'

'Uh-uh, at the other end of the hall, in front of the main exit,' he said.

Alicia was unusually quiet. She looked nervous. I looked her in the eye, wanting her to say something but she didn't. Then I started off, moving slowly

17 **to split up** to separate into parts or groups – 25 **traffic jam** a situation in which a long line of vehicles have stopped moving or are moving very slowly

along the wall, scanning faces. There were many small groups and I had to move around them to get a better look. Another problem was that many of the guys had on leather jackets like the one Ritchie was wearing.

All the while I was searching, my mind was searching, too. Searching for an answer to the question, where had Ritchie gone? Many thoughts raced through my mind. One of them kept coming back. But I didn't want to think that thought and kept pushing it away.

I continued on, moving faster now as the crowd grew smaller. When I finally reached the other end of the hall, Rico and Scooter were already there. I could see Alicia approaching from the other side.

'Well?' Scooter said to me.

'Nothing,' I said, shrugging my shoulders. 'And you two?'

'Nada,' said Rico.

We turned to Alicia. She shook her head. 'The answer is no,' she said with a twisted smile.

'What about Jackson? Anyone seen him?' Alicia asked.

'He'll show up soon. We'll wait for him,' Scooter said.

I turned to Scooter again. 'Did you notice the blonde in the first row?'

'Who didn't notice her?' he said, grinning at Rico and Jackson.

'Ritchie did, that's for sure,' I said.

Scooter grinned but said nothing.

'That was gross – the way he flirted with her.'

1 **to scan** to look at sth carefully in order to find sb or sth – 17 **to shrug** to raise and lower your shoulders to show you do not know or care about sth – 19 **nada** the Spanish word for 'nothing'

'Yeah,' said Alicia. 'First he reaches down and gives her his hand, then he kisses her.'

Scooter nodded, still grinning.

I looked at Rico and Jackson. They were grinning, too. 'No comments?' I said. 'Aren't you guys a little surprised? I mean – he's Alicia's boyfriend after all.'

More silent grinning.

I looked at them and waited.

A long moment went by, then Scooter shook his head. 'Surprised? Not really. We know Ritchie. We've been in his band a couple of years now.'

'Look!' a voice came from behind us. 'They're in that great rapper band!' We turned around. Five or six kids were zeroing in on us. 'Amazing music!' said one of them. 'Great stuff,' said another. 'Loved those raps,' said a third.

'Hey, thanks,' said Scooter, fist-bumping the group as they went by. We did the same.

When they were gone, I turned to Scooter again. 'You said, "We know Ritchie". What exactly did you mean by that?'

14 **to zero in** to aim directly at sb or sth – 17 **to fist-bump** two or more people hit their tightly closed hands together to show that they are friends

Scooter looked at me as if I were a child. 'Duh, Ritchie's a good-looking guy. Girls find him, er, attractive.'

'And he finds girls attractive, too. Is that it?'

Scooter nodded. 'Too true,' he said.

My eyes flashed. 'But there's more to it than that, isn't there?' I waited for him to answer but he didn't. 'Well?' I said in a sharp voice.

'Alicia wasn't his first girlfriend – ,' he began.

'Not his second or third, either!' Alicia said.

Rico and Jackson were grinning again. 'You're right about that!' Rico said.

'We're beginning to get the picture,' I said. 'We're talking hit-and-run here, are we?'

Rico and Jackson nodded. Scooter seemed to want to say something but then he only nodded, too..

I thought for a moment. 'Well, why didn't you warn us – er, I mean Alicia?'

Scooter gave me a strange look. 'Warn Alicia? Ha! She's a big girl. She don't need no warnings.'

I looked at Alicia. She was very calm. She nodded slowly and said, 'That's right. I don't need any warnings. I can take care of myself.' She paused a moment. 'I'm not blind. I knew that Ritchie likes to flirt. I accepted that. Still, when it happens, especially right in front of my nose like this, it hurts.'

I put my hand on her shoulder. I felt sorry for her – and for me!

Scooter turned and looked me in the eye. There was a little smile on his face. 'Maybe you're the one that needed the warning,' he said.

14 **hit-and-run** a quick action by sb who then leaves or runs away quickly

16
Hit and run man

I felt my face growing warm. ‘Me? What have I got to do with it?’ I said in a loud voice.

Scooter’s smile turned into a broad grin. ‘I can’t prove it, but it wouldn’t surprise me if you fell under Ritchie’s spell, too.’

I let out a nervous laugh. Alicia gave me a sharp look. ‘Me - under Ritchie’s spell? You must be dreaming!’

Scooter gave Rico and Jackson a knowing smile. They began to giggle. ‘Maybe I am,’ he said slowly, ‘but from what I’ve seen, you certainly enjoy being around him.’

Aware that they were all staring at me, I searched for something to say. ‘I – I feel sorry for him,’ I said quickly.

‘Sorry? For Ritchie?’ Scooter said in an are-you-crazy? tone of voice.

I hesitated, not sure where my words were taking me. I felt like a diver on a high rock looking down at the dark water below. ‘He told me about his mother.’

Alicia’s eyes were all over my face. She seemed about to say something but she suddenly looked away.

‘What about his mother?’ Scooter had me in a corner now and wasn’t about to let me go.

Just then, two security men came over to us. They were closing down the hall now, they said, and we’d have to leave.

6 **to fall under sb’s spell** when you ~ , you become so fascinated by them that you can’t think of anything else – 12 **to giggle** to laugh in a nervous or childlike way – 15 **aware** [ə'wer] knowing that sth exists – 19 **tone** the quality of a person’s voice – 29 **security man** person who guards a place to make sure the people and things there are safe

Saved by the bell, I thought, as we headed for the exit. But as soon as we reached the parking lot outside, Scooter started in again. He was enjoying this too much to stop now. 'What did Ritchie tell you about his mother?'

Again I felt the stares. I hesitated, searching for the right words. 'He said Mattapan was making his mother sick, so sick she hardly left her apartment any more. He was trying to earn enough money with his music to move from Mattapan to a place where there was less noise and crime, where she could get well again.'

Scooter, Rico and Jackson exchanged knowing smiles. Scooter shook his head and gave me a look of fake surprise. 'And you believed him?'

My heart started beating fast. I glanced over at Alicia. She was staring at me, open-mouthed. 'Yes,' I said quickly.

'Well, let me tell you something. Ritchie loves Mattapan and he'd never move away. No way! Ditto for his mother. I know Mrs. Timmins and I know that she loves Mattapan just as much as Ritchie does. As for her being sick – that's bullshit! She's fitter than I'll ever be!'

My mouth fell open. I nodded slowly, playing for time. My survival instinct told me: play dumb, it's your only chance! 'I – I don't understand,' I said softly, putting on a helpless-little-girl look.

Scooter stood staring at me, thinking about what I'd said. 'Why would he tell you a thing like that?' he began slowly. 'Knowing Ritchie,' he went on

1 **saved by the bell** sth you say when a difficult situation is ended suddenly before you have to do or say sth you do not want to – 15 **fake** [feɪk] not true or real – 16 **to glance** [glænts] to look at sb or sth very quickly – 23 **bullshit** *inf* silly or untrue words or ideas – 26 **to play dumb** [dʌm] to act as if you didn't know sth

after a short pause, 'it has to be because he wanted something from you. But what?'

'I don't know,' I said.

'He wanted you to feel sorry for him – is that it?'

Rico smiled at Scooter. 'Yeah. To get her to hook up with him.'

Jackson shook his head. 'That don't sound right. Normally, all Ritchie has to do is snap his finger and the girls come running. He don't have to make up stories like that!'

Scooter nodded slowly, his eyes fixed on mine. 'Well, Sarah?' he said after a while. 'What's the story – the real story? You're holding something back, aren't you? Come on, spit it out!'

5 **to hook up with** *sl* to have a romantic relationship with – 8 **to snap** to use thumb and fingers to make a short, sharp sound – 14 **spit it out** *inf* used to tell sb to say sth that they don't want to say

17
Welcome to the real world

I lowered my head. My heart was pounding. My throat was dry. Scooter had a twisted grin on his face. He had me now, and he knew it. I was just about to speak when Alicia put her hand on my shoulder and smiled at me. 'What is it, Sarah? You can say it. I'm on your side.'

I looked her in the eye and began slowly. 'As you know, Ritchie was flirting with me. Stupid me, I thought it was more than just a flirt. I had a talk with him to find out where I stood. He said he liked me but he was in a very stressful situation. He had to concentrate on his music, he said. He had to earn enough money to move out of Mattapan because of what it was doing to his mother.' I studied Alicia's eyes to see what effect my words were having on her.

Her smile was gone, but she nodded.

'And, of course, you were his girlfriend. He didn't want to hurt you. He asked me to please try to understand his situation and not do anything to make things more difficult for him.'

'Ha!' Scooter cried. 'That's Ritchie! Wanting two girlfriends at the same time. Having his cake and eating it, too!'

'Yeah, he sure likes cake,' laughed Rico.

'The more the better!' Jackson started laughing, too.

I looked at Alicia. Her eyes were flashing with anger.

'I hope he chokes on it!' she said.

4 **throat** the tube inside the neck that leads to the stomach and lungs – 25 **to have your cake and eat it, too** *coll* to do or get two good things at the same time – 32 **to choke** to have serious problems with your breathing *(ersticken)*

'Ouch!' Scooter's face twisted in fake shock.

Just then, a shout came from the dark end of the parking lot. 'Hey! There you are!' A moment later, Ritchie appeared, grinning from ear to ear. 'Okay, guys,' he said in a loud voice. 'Are you ready for the disco?' He let out a strange, wild laugh.

'Where were you?' said Alicia flatly.

Ritchie's grin vanished. 'Oh, uh, I couldn't find my wallet. I thought I might have forgotten it in the van.'

'And – was it there?' There was a note of amusement in Alicia's voice.

'Yep. Under the seat, where I left it.'

'Good for you! Did the blonde help you look for it?'

Ritchie's mouth fell open. He gave Scooter a what's-this-all-about? look. Scooter looked away. 'Blonde? What blonde?'

'The one you were flirting with in the front row,' Alicia said in a cool voice.

Ritchie's eyes narrowed. 'Blonde in the front row?'

Alicia stayed calm. 'Have you forgotten her already? The one you flirted with all during our show.'

Ritchie laughed nervously. 'Oh, her. Hey, that was nothing, just part of my performance, that's all. Something my fans expect of me. I have to do it.'

I had to laugh. 'Sure, Ritchie. It belongs to your image. You've got to keep up your image, right?'

Ritchie forced a smile but said nothing.

Alicia shook her head. 'Does it also belong to your image to continue flirting after the show?'

'Now what's that supposed to mean?'

8 **to vanish** to disappear – 9 **wallet** [ˈwɑːlɪt] a small folding case that holds money, credit cards, etc

'You know exactly what it means. You should have taken a look at yourself in the car mirror before coming here. Look at you! Your hair's all messed up, and what's that red mark on the side of your face?'

Ritchie let out a nervous laugh. 'Hey, what's this? The girl wanted to have a little fun, that's all. She got me to go to her car with her. She said she had some photos she wanted to show me. I – '

I let out a loud laugh. 'Come on! You can do better than that!' I said, frowning at him. 'Do you really think we're dumb enough to believe crap like that?'

Suddenly, he started laughing, too. When he finished, he nodded his head slowly and fixed his eyes on Alicia and me. 'Welcome to the real world, girls,' he said. 'It's maybe not as nice as you thought but it's real. It's where I'm at. It's me, Ritchie T, the real Ritchie T!'

'The real Ritchie T? You mean the one with the sick mother, the one who's doing everything to make enough money to move away from Mattapan?'

Ritchie shot an angry look at Scooter, then grinned, trying to hide his shock. He nodded. 'Yep. That's the one.'

Alicia looked at me, rolling her eyes. I turned to Ritchie. 'You're so noble, a real prince, you know that?' I said, my words heavy with irony.

'Hey, come on,' he said with a shrug. 'Nobody's perfect, okay?'

'No, not okay,' I said. 'Not the way you've used us.'

'What? Haven't I used you well? I made you part of the band, didn't I? You're having fun, aren't you? You want to stay in the band, don't you?'

2 **mirror** [ˈmɪrɚ] *Spiegel* – 3 **messed up** dirty, untidy – 21 **to shoot a look** to look quickly and suddenly – 26 **irony** the use of words to mean the opposite of what you really think

Alicia shook her head, a little ironic smile on her face. 'Nice try, Ritchie. But no thanks. We don't want to be part of your band any more.'

'Hey, come on,' Ritchie said with a laugh. 'You're taking this too seriously. You're upset. I can understand that. But listen – you'll get over it. Tomorrow's another day. Come on. You're big girls. Say yes.' He gave us a cocky grin.

'No' said Alicia quickly.

I made him wait for my answer. Finally, I looked him square in the eye, smiled and said, 'No way!'

The cocky grin vanished. For a long moment, Ritchie's eyes searched Alicia's face, then mine. 'Is that your last word?' he said in a weak voice.

'Yes, it is, but hey – ' I said with a bright fake smile, 'knowing you, you'll have no problem replacing us, right? For you, girls like us are dime a dozen.'

Ritchie glanced at Scooter, then he turned back to us, shaking his head, his eyes full of fake pity. 'Too bad, but all right, if that's what you want, it's your decision. I can't force you to stay.'

Alicia let out a laugh. 'Too bad – no, you can't,' she said sarcastically. 'And if you ask me, replacing us won't be that easy.' Smiling at me, she added, 'You and I were good, Sarah, really good.'

'Definitely!' I said, straight-faced.

Ritchie was about to say something but before he could get the words out, I took Alicia by the hand and said, 'Come on, Alicia. Let's go home.'

Without another word we turned and, hand in hand, began walking away, leaving Ritchie and the others staring, shaking their heads, and watching us go.

8 **cocky** having or showing confidence in a way that makes other people angry –
17 **dime a dozen** *coll* if a thing is very common and easy to get, you can say it is a ~ –
19 **pity** ['pɪt̬i] a strong feeling of sadness for sth or sb

Class activities

CHAPTER 1

In pairs, think about what Sarah means when she describes Alicia as a 'sleepwalker on top of a high building'.

a) Using your own words, explain what she means.
b) Think up your own simile to describe the situation Alicia is in. ("She / It is like …)

CHAPTER 2

In groups of three, study the text and prepare a performance. Half of the groups prepare to perform the first part of the scene (up to where Alicia throws herself in Ritchie's arms, page 12, line 9), the other half prepares the second part, from *Ritchie held her a moment …* to the end.

CHAPTER 3

In pairs, discuss what Sarah means when she says '*I'd crossed that line.*'

a) Explain what she means.
b) Think up a similar situation in which someone 'crosses the line'.

CHAPTER 4

In groups, prepare to perform Ritchie's rap about love. Or, one group could be the jury and choose what they think are the two best performances for the final.
The other groups could then vote on which of the two finalists give the better performance.

CHAPTER 5

In groups of six or seven, study the four scenes of the video production and prepare to perform them. Three or four students do the rap, while three others – as Sarah, Alicia and Ritchie – act out the scenes.

CHAPTER 6

In pairs, study the scene, one student concentrating on Alicia's accusation that Sarah flirted with her boyfriend, the other on Sarah's response that she didn't really mean anything by it. Then put aside the text and role-play the scene. Feel free to use your own words.

CHAPTER 7

Sarah's worries about meeting Ritchie alone in Mattapan cause her to have a frightening daydream. Working in pairs, think up a similar daydream Sarah might have had. Be prepared to share your results with the class.

CHAPTER 8

Working in pairs, take a close look at the last part of the chapter about the rumors at school about Ritchie. Create a scene in which school kids are talking about why Ritchie dropped out of school.

CHAPTER 9

Try to imagine
a) you are Ritchie's mother watching Ritchie and a girl (Sarah) from your window;
b) you are Sarah on your way home from Mattapan thinking about what Ritchie said about himself and his mother.
Write down what you think Ritchie's mother and Sarah are thinking.

CHAPTER 10

Rap contest! Form groups and prepare to perform Ritchie's rap, Mattapan. One of the groups is the jury, whose job it is to decide which group has performed the best. The winning group repeats their performance.

CHAPTER 11

Working in groups of six, act out the rap as described in the text. As Ritchie, one member of the group does the rap while the others play the different parts.

CHAPTER 12

Internet project: Working in pairs, search the internet for information on Boston, focussing on what is said about the quality of life (or lack of it) in Boston. Prepare to explain why you agree or disagree with the negative picture of Boston Sarah paints in her rap.

CHAPTER 13

Read through chapter thirteen twice, then put your book aside and complete the following sentences:

Alicia stayed ____

____.

I missed him, too, ____________________________________

____.

We were like boxers ___________________________________

____

____.

Quoting Ritchie _______________________________________

____.

All at once, she reached ______________________________

____.

The cafeteria, which was ______________________________

____.

____.

On one was ____

____

____.

Suddenly, the cafeteria _______________________________

____.

CHAPTER 14

Read through the chapter carefully, then put your book aside.
Five of the following statements are false. Can you find and correct them?

1) Silver Mountain, a popular local band, got the concert off to a good start.

____

____

2) Ritchie didn't have to work hard to get the attention of the audience.

____

____

3) Ritchie said the first rap was about the land he loved.

____

____

4) Ritchie's rap about the U.S.A. ends with the question, 'What are you doing, America?'

____

____